SELF ESTEEM FOR WOMEN

Thriving In Adversity

Kira Shawn

TABLE OF CONTENT

INTRODUCTION

Welcome to your journey towards self-esteem and empowerment!

This book is here to guide you through understanding, building, and maintaining your self-esteem in a way that's not just insightful but also exciting.

Self-esteem isn't just about feeling good; it's about recognizing your worth, embracing your strengths, and facing life's challenges with confidence and joy.

Self-esteem is crucial for every aspect of your life. It influences how you see yourself and how you interact with others.

When you have healthy self-esteem, you're more likely to pursue your dreams, set boundaries, and live a fulfilling life.

Low self-esteem, on the other hand, can hold you back, making you doubt your abilities and accept less than you deserve.

This book is designed to make your personal growth journey thrilling.

Personal growth doesn't have to be dull or tedious

It can be an exciting adventure filled with new discoveries about yourself, thrilling achievements, and empowering moments.

Think of it as an adventure where each step forward brings you closer to the confident, empowered woman you aspire to be.

As you dive into this book, you'll learn practical strategies to boost your self-esteem, overcome obstacles, and build a life you love.

Let's embark on this exciting journey together, transforming your self-esteem and unleashing your full potential!

Self-esteem is simply how you feel about yourself.

It's the overall sense of self-worth and value you have as a person.

Think of self-esteem as the foundation of your mental and emotional well-being.

When your self-esteem is strong, you feel confident, capable, and worthy.

When it's weak, you might struggle with feelings of inadequacy and self-doubt.

Self-esteem impacts every area of your life.

It influences your relationships, career, and how you handle stress and setbacks.

When you have healthy self-esteem, you're more likely to set boundaries, pursue your goals, and cope with challenges effectively.

Conversely, low self-esteem can lead to self-sabotage, unhealthy relationships, and missed opportunities.

Understanding self-esteem begins with recognizing that it's not about perfection.

It's about accepting yourself as you are, with all your strengths and weaknesses. It's about believing that you are deserving of love, respect, and happiness.

This belief forms the bedrock of your self-esteem.

The Psychology Behind Self-Worth
Understanding why we feel the way we do about ourselves can help us make positive changes.

Our self-esteem often develops from a young age, influenced by our family, friends, and experiences.

Positive experiences and supportive relationships tend to boost self-esteem, while negative experiences and criticism can harm it.

Several factors shape our self-esteem

–The way we are treated by our parents, teachers, and peers in childhood has a lasting impact. Supportive, loving relationships foster high self-esteem, while neglect, criticism, or abuse can damage it.

–We often compare ourselves to others, and this can affect our self-esteem. If we perceive ourselves as falling short compared to others, our self-worth can suffer.

–Successes and failures, achievements, and setbacks all play a role. Overcoming challenges and achieving goals can boost self-esteem, while repeated failures can erode it.

–The way we talk to ourselves matters. Positive self-talk can enhance self-esteem, while negative self-talk can undermine it. Recognizing and challenging negative thoughts is crucial.

But here's the good news: self-esteem isn't fixed. You have the power to change how you see yourself, no matter your past.

By understanding the psychology behind self-worth, you can start to rewire your thoughts and beliefs to support a healthier, more positive self-image.

Myths and Facts About Self-Esteem
There are many myths about self-esteem that can mislead us. Let's clear up some common misconceptions:

-**Myth:** High self-esteem means being arrogant or self-centered.
-**Fact:** True self-esteem is about feeling good about yourself while also respecting

and valuing others. It's about balance, not arrogance.

-**Myth:** Self-esteem is based on accomplishments.
-**Fact:** While achievements can boost your confidence, self-esteem comes from within. It's about recognizing your inherent worth, regardless of external successes.

-**Myth:** You're either born with self-esteem or you're not.
 -**Fact:** Self-esteem can be developed and strengthened over time.
It's not something you're stuck with; it's something you can work on and improve.

-**Myth:** Only certain people deserve to have high self-esteem.
-**Fact:** Everyone deserves to feel good about themselves. Self-esteem is not a privilege; it's a right.

-**Myth:** High self-esteem solves all your problems.

-Fact: While healthy self-esteem can improve your quality of life, it's not a magic solution to all challenges. It's one important piece of overall well-being.

Understanding these truths can help you approach your journey to better self-esteem with a clear, informed perspective.

In building your self-esteem,where do you start from?
Improving your self-esteem is a journey, and every journey begins with a single step.

Take time to reflect on your strengths, achievements, and qualities. Write them down and revisit this list often.

This helps you focus on the positive aspects of yourself.

Pay attention to your inner dialogue.

Challenge negative thoughts and replace them with positive affirmations. For example, if you catch yourself thinking, "I can't do this," reframe it to, "I am capable and can handle this."

Setting and achieving small, realistic goals can boost your confidence.

Break down large goals into manageable steps, and celebrate your progress along the way.

Taking care of your physical, emotional, and mental health is crucial.

Ensure you get enough rest, eat well, exercise, and engage in activities that bring you joy.

Spend time with people who uplift and support you.

Avoid those who bring negativity or criticism into your life.

Positive relationships are key to maintaining healthy self-esteem.

Setting boundaries is essential for protecting your self-esteem.

Don't be afraid to say no to things that don't serve your well-being or align with your values.

Regularly practice gratitude by acknowledging the good things in your life.

This shifts your focus from what's lacking to what's abundant, fostering a positive outlook.

If your self-esteem issues are deeply rooted and difficult to manage, consider seeking help from a therapist or counselor.

Professional support can provide valuable insights and strategies.

Building self-esteem is a continuous process.

There will be ups and downs, but each step forward is progress.

Embrace the journey with patience and compassion for yourself.

Remember that it's okay to seek help and that you don't have to do it alone.

Negative influences come in various forms and can significantly impact your self-esteem.

These influences can be external, such as critical comments from others, or internal, such as self-criticism and negative self-talk.

External Influences

People who frequently criticize or belittle you can damage your self-esteem.

These individuals might be friends, family members, colleagues, or even strangers.

Their negative comments can make you doubt your abilities and worth.

Being in a toxic relationship, whether romantic, familial, or platonic, can erode your self-esteem over time.

Toxic relationships often involve manipulation, control, and emotional abuse, leading you to feel unworthy and powerless.

Society and media often set unrealistic standards of beauty, success, and behavior.

Constantly comparing yourself to these ideals can make you feel inadequate and lower your self-esteem.

Internal Influences

The way you talk to yourself significantly impacts your self-esteem.

Negative self-talk involves harshly criticizing yourself, focusing on your flaws, and doubting your abilities.

This internal dialogue can be more damaging than external criticism.

Striving for perfection can lead to constant disappointment and self-criticism.

Perfectionism sets unattainable standards, making it impossible to feel good about your achievements and progress.

Fear of failure can prevent you from taking risks and pursuing your goals.

This fear often stems from a belief that your worth is tied to your success, leading to anxiety and self-doubt.

Societal pressures can be overwhelming, but understanding and addressing them can help you maintain a healthy self-esteem.

Recognize that societal standards are often unrealistic and unattainable.

Remind yourself that everyone has flaws and imperfections, and that's what makes us human.

Celebrate your uniqueness and focus on your strengths rather than trying to meet impossible standards.

Be mindful of the media you consume.

Follow accounts and consume content that promotes body positivity, self-love, and authenticity. Unfollow accounts that make you feel inadequate or promote unrealistic ideals.

Surround yourself with people who uplift and support you.

Seek out relationships that encourage self-acceptance and celebrate your achievements. Positive influences can counteract societal pressures and reinforce your self-worth.

Treat yourself with the same kindness and understanding you would offer a friend. Acknowledge that everyone makes mistakes and has bad days.

Practicing self-compassion helps you navigate societal pressures with resilience and grace.

Your inner critic is that voice inside your head that judges, criticizes, and undermines you. Learning to manage and quiet this voice is essential for building self-esteem.

The first step in dealing with your inner critic is to recognize when it's speaking. Pay attention to negative thoughts and self-critical comments.

Awareness is key to addressing and challenging these thoughts.

Once you recognize your inner critic, challenge its validity.

Ask yourself if the criticism is based on facts or assumptions. Replace negative thoughts with more balanced and realistic ones.

For example, if your inner critic says, "You'll never succeed," counter it with, "I have the skills and determination to succeed."

Replace negative self-talk with positive affirmations. Affirmations are positive statements that reinforce your self-worth and abilities.

For example, say to yourself, "I am capable and deserving of success," or "I am worthy of love and respect."

Sometimes, our inner critic can be irrational and overly harsh. Seek feedback from trusted friends, family, or colleagues to gain a more balanced perspective.

Their positive feedback can help counteract your inner critic and boost your self-esteem.

Engage in activities that make you feel confident and competent. Whether it's a hobby, exercise, or volunteering, doing things you enjoy and excel at can counteract negative self-talk and build your self-esteem.

Resilience is the ability to bounce back from setbacks and challenges. Building resilience is essential for maintaining healthy self-esteem, especially when faced with obstacles.

Embrace a growth mindset, which is the belief that you can learn and grow from challenges. View setbacks as opportunities for growth rather than failures.

This mindset shift can help you approach obstacles with a positive attitude and build resilience.

Taking care of your physical, emotional, and mental well-being is crucial for building resilience.

Ensure you get enough rest, eat nutritious foods, exercise regularly, and engage in activities that bring you joy and relaxation.

Surround yourself with supportive and positive people.

A strong support network can provide encouragement, advice, and a sense of belonging during difficult times.

Reflect on past setbacks and what you learned from them. Identify the skills and strengths you gained from overcoming challenges.

This reflection can help you see setbacks as opportunities for growth and build resilience.

Focus on the positive aspects of your life and practice gratitude.

Keeping a gratitude journal can help you recognize and appreciate the good things in your life, which can boost your resilience and overall well-being.

Toxic relationships can significantly impact your self-esteem. Learning to recognize and navigate these relationships is crucial for protecting your self-worth.

Toxic relationships often involve manipulation, control, and emotional abuse. Recognize the signs of a toxic relationship, such as constant criticism, lack of support, and feeling drained or unworthy.

Setting boundaries is essential for protecting your self-esteem. Clearly communicate your needs and limits, and enforce them consistently. Boundaries help you maintain your self-respect and prevent others from taking advantage of you.

Talk to trusted friends, family, or a therapist about the toxic relationship. Their support and guidance can help you navigate the situation and make informed decisions.

Reflect on whether the relationship is worth maintaining. Sometimes, it's necessary to distance yourself from toxic individuals to protect your well-being and self-esteem.

Invest in relationships that uplift and support you. Positive relationships reinforce your self-worth and provide a healthy environment for growth and self-esteem.

Change can be challenging but embracing it is essential for personal growth and building self-esteem. Learning to navigate and adapt to change can boost your confidence and resilience.

Change can bring up a range of emotions, from excitement to fear. Acknowledge and validate your feelings rather than suppressing them. Understanding your emotions can help you navigate change more effectively.

involves focusing on the good in your life and adopting a hopeful and optimistic attitude.

Regularly practice gratitude by acknowledging the good things in your life. Keeping a gratitude journal can help you focus on the positive aspects and shift your mindset from scarcity to abundance.

Surround yourself with positive influences, whether it's people, books, or media. Positive influences can uplift your mood and reinforce a positive mindset.

When faced with challenges, focus on finding solutions rather than dwelling on problems. A solution-focused approach helps you stay proactive and optimistic.

Mindfulness involves staying present and fully engaging in the moment. Practicing mindfulness can help you reduce stress, improve your focus, and cultivate a positive mindset.

Engage in activities that bring you joy and fulfillment.

Whether it's a hobby, exercise, or spending time with loved ones, positive activities can boost your mood and reinforce a positive mindset.

Building self-esteem involves embracing and accepting your true self. This means recognizing your unique qualities, strengths, and imperfections and loving yourself unconditionally.

Take time to reflect on your values, passions, and strengths. Understanding what makes you unique can help you embrace your true self and build self-esteem.

Be true to yourself in your actions and interactions. Authenticity involves expressing your true thoughts and feelings rather than conforming to others' expectations.

Embracing authenticity can boost your confidence and self-worth needed to thrive. Embrace each step of your journey, knowing that every effort you make to understand and improve yourself is valuable. Let's summarize the key takeaways from this chapter to solidify your understanding and prepare you for the next steps.

In this chapter, we'll explore simple, everyday practices you can incorporate into your life to build and strengthen your self-esteem. These practices are easy to understand and can make a big difference in how you feel about yourself.

Morning Rituals: Starting Your Day Right

How you start your day can set the tone for everything that follows. Creating a morning routine that focuses on positivity and self-care can help you begin each day feeling confident and energized.

Giving yourself enough time in the morning helps reduce stress and allows you to start your day calmly. Waking up early ensures you have time to focus on yourself before diving into daily tasks.

Before getting out of bed, think of three things you're grateful for. They can be simple, like having a comfortable bed, or more profound, like your health or relationships. This practice helps shift your mindset to one of appreciation and positivity.

Physical activity releases endorphins, which are chemicals in your brain that make you feel good. A short stretch or exercise routine in the morning can boost your mood and energy levels for the day ahead.

Fueling your body with nutritious food sets a positive tone for the day. Choose foods that provide energy and keep you feeling full and focused.

Decide what you want to focus on for the day. It could be something like being patient, staying positive, or working towards a specific goal. Setting an intention helps direct your energy and attention positively.

Mindfulness and Meditation: Finding Inner Peace

Mindfulness and meditation are powerful tools for calming your mind and building self-awareness. These practices help you stay present and reduce stress, which can positively impact your self-esteem.

Take a few minutes each day to focus on your breath. Sit comfortably, close your eyes, and take slow, deep breaths. Pay attention to the sensation of your breath entering and leaving your body. This simple practice can help you feel grounded and centered.

Body Scan Meditation:This involves focusing on different parts of your body, one at a time, and noticing any sensations you feel. Start at your toes and work your way up to your head. This practice helps you become more aware of your body and can reduce tension and stress.

Spend a few minutes meditating on things you're grateful for. Imagine each thing in your mind and focus on the positive feelings they bring. This practice helps reinforce a positive mindset.

Pay full attention to your food as you eat. Notice the colors, textures, and flavors. Eating mindfully can help you appreciate your meals more and make healthier choices.

Loving-Kindness Meditation: This practice involves sending positive thoughts to yourself and others. Start by silently repeating phrases like "May I be happy, may I be healthy, may I be safe." Then extend these wishes to others, including loved ones and even people you find challenging. This meditation helps cultivate compassion and positivity.

Affirmations and Visualization: Harnessing Positive Thinking

Affirmations and visualization are techniques that use the power of positive thinking to boost your confidence and self-esteem. They help you focus on your strengths and goals.

Write down a few positive statements about yourself and repeat them daily. Examples include "I am capable," "I deserve happiness," and "I am strong." Say them out loud or silently to reinforce these beliefs.

A vision board is a collection of images and words that represent your goals and dreams. It can be a poster, a digital collage, or even a notebook. Looking at your vision board regularly reminds you of what you're working towards and keeps you motivated.

Spend a few minutes each day imagining yourself achieving your goals. Picture the steps you'll take and the feelings you'll experience. Visualization helps make your goals feel more real and attainable.

Replace negative thoughts with positive ones. When you catch yourself thinking something negative, like "I can't do this," reframe it to "I can handle this" or "I will try my best." This shift in thinking can improve your self-confidence.

Write your affirmations on small cards and place them where you'll see them throughout the day, such as your mirror, fridge, or workspace. These reminders help keep your mind focused on positive thoughts.

Self-Care Routines: Prioritizing Your Well-Being
Self-care is all about taking time to care for yourself physically, emotionally, and mentally. Prioritizing self-care helps you feel more balanced and capable.

Engage in activities that keep your body healthy and strong. This includes regular exercise, getting enough sleep, eating nutritious foods, and staying hydrated.

Physical health has a direct impact on your mood and energy levels.

Pay attention to your emotions and find healthy ways to express them. This might involve talking to a friend, writing in a journal, or practicing relaxation techniques like deep breathing or yoga.

Stimulate your mind with activities that challenge and interest you. Read books, solve puzzles, learn something new, or engage in creative activities like drawing or playing music.

Spend time with people who make you feel good about yourself. Building strong, positive relationships provides support and boosts your self-esteem. Make time for social activities and connect with loved ones regularly.

Connect with your inner self and find activities that bring you a sense of peace and purpose. This could be meditation, spending time in nature, praying, or engaging in a creative hobby. Spiritual self-care helps you feel grounded and centered.

Journaling: Reflecting on Your Thoughts and Progress

Journaling is a powerful way to reflect on your thoughts, track your progress, and express your emotions. It can help you gain insights into yourself and your journey.

Set aside time each day to write in your journal. Reflect on your experiences, emotions, and any challenges you faced. Writing helps you process your thoughts and can provide clarity.

Keep a separate journal where you write down things you're grateful for each day. Focusing on gratitude can improve your mood and help you appreciate the positive aspects of your life

Track your progress towards your goals. Write about the steps you've taken, any

obstacles you've overcome, and your achievements. Celebrating your progress, no matter how small, boosts your confidence.
Record your daily moods and any factors that might be influencing them. This can help you identify patterns and understand what affects your emotions. Understanding your moods can help you manage them better.

Use your journal to visualize and plan for the future. Write about your dreams, aspirations, and the steps you'll take to achieve them. This practice helps you stay focused and motivated.

Setting Intentions: Focusing Your Energy
Setting intentions involves deciding what you want to focus on and achieve. It helps direct your energy and attention towards positive outcomes.

Each morning, take a moment to set an intention for the day. It could be something simple like "I will be kind to myself" or "I will focus on my work." Setting intentions helps you start your day with purpose and direction.

At the beginning of each week, set intentions for what you want to achieve. These might be related to work, personal growth, or relationships. Review your intentions regularly to stay on track

At the start of each month, reflect on your long-term goals and set intentions for the month. This practice helps you stay focused on your bigger picture and make consistent progress.

Set intentions for specific events or challenges. For example, if you have a big presentation at work, your intention might be "I will stay calm and confident." Setting intentions for specific situations can help you approach them with a positive mindset.

At the end of the day, week, or month, reflect on your intentions and how they influenced your actions and experiences. This reflection helps you understand your progress and adjust your intentions as needed.

Gratitude Practices: Cultivating Abundance

Practicing gratitude helps you focus on the positive aspects of your life and fosters a sense of abundance and appreciation.

Each day, write down three things you're grateful for. They can be simple, like a sunny day, or more significant, like a supportive friend. This practice shifts your focus to the positive aspects of your life.

Write a letter to someone you're grateful for. Express your appreciation for their presence in your life and how they've impacted you. You don't have to send the letter, but writing it helps you feel more connected and appreciative.

Keep a jar where you drop in notes about things you're grateful for. Over time, the jar will fill up with positive memories and reminders. When you're feeling down, read through the notes to boost your mood.

Spend a few minutes each day meditating on things you're grateful for. Visualize them in your mind and focus on the positive feelings they bring. This meditation reinforces a sense of abundance.

Take a walk and focus on the things you're grateful for along the way. It could be the beauty of nature, the kindness of strangers, or the opportunity to move and enjoy the outdoors.

This practice combines physical activity with mindfulness and gratitude, enhancing your overall well-being.

Setting thrilling goals is essential for building self-esteem and creating a sense of purpose and direction in your life.

Goals provide a roadmap for your personal and professional development, helping you focus on what truly matters and motivating you to take action.

In this chapter, we will work on the importance of goal setting, how to create **S.M.A.R.T.** goals, and ways to overcome fear and doubt that might hold you back.

Goals are powerful tools that can transform your life. They give you a sense of purpose and direction, helping you to stay focused and motivated. Here's why goal setting is so important:

Goals provide clarity on what you want to achieve. They help you focus your energy and resources on activities that align with your aspirations.

Goals serve as a source of motivation and inspiration. They give you something to strive for, keeping you driven and enthusiastic.

Goals allow you to track your progress and see how far you've come. This can be incredibly rewarding and reinforces your commitment.

Accomplishing goals boosts your self-esteem and confidence. Each goal achieved is a testament to your hard work and dedication.

Setting and pursuing goals challenges you to grow and develop. It pushes you out of your comfort zone and encourages continuous improvement.

Creating S.M.A.R.T. Goals

Effective goal setting involves creating S.M.A.R.T. goals.

S.M.A.R.T. stands for Specific, Measurable, Achievable, Relevant, and Time-bound. This framework ensures that your goals are clear and attainable.
Your goals should be clear and specific. Instead of saying, "I want to improve my self-esteem," say, "I want to increase my self-confidence by attending a self-development workshop."

Ensure your goals are measurable so you can track your progress. For example, "I want to read two self-help books per month."

Set realistic goals that you can achieve. Consider your current abilities and resources. A goal like "I want to start a daily meditation practice for 10 minutes" is more achievable than an unrealistic one.

Your goals should align with your values and long-term objectives. Ensure that each goal is meaningful and contributes to your overall growth. For example, if you value health, a relevant goal might be, "I want to exercise three times a week."

Set a deadline for your goals. Having a timeframe creates a sense of urgency and helps you stay focused. For example, "I want to complete an online course on self-esteem within three months."

Example of a S.M.A.R.T. Goal

-Specific: I want to increase my self-esteem by completing a public speaking course.

-Measurable: I will measure my progress by giving a presentation in front of an audience.

-Achievable: I will enroll in a beginner-level course that meets once a week.

-Relevant: Improving my public speaking skills will boost my confidence and self-esteem.

-Time-bound: I will complete the course within three months.

Overcoming Fear and Doubt

Fear and doubt are common obstacles that can prevent you from setting and achieving your goals. Here are some strategies to overcome these barriers:

Acknowledge what you're afraid of. Is it fear of failure, rejection, or the unknown? Understanding your fears is the first step to overcoming them.

Replace negative thoughts with positive affirmations. Instead of thinking, "I can't do this," tell yourself, "I am capable and worthy of success."

Large goals can be overwhelming. Break them down into smaller, manageable steps. This makes the process less daunting and more achievable.

Surround yourself with supportive people who encourage and believe in you. Share your goals with them and ask for their support.

Visualization is a powerful tool. Imagine yourself achieving your goals and experiencing the positive outcomes. This can boost your confidence and motivation.

Start taking small steps towards your goals, even if you feel uncertain. Action builds momentum and reduces fear.

Understand that failure is a part of the learning process. If you encounter setbacks, use them as opportunities to learn and grow.

Be kind to yourself. Recognize that everyone experiences fear and doubt. Treat yourself with compassion and understanding.

Example of Overcoming Fear

-**Fear:** "I'm afraid of speaking in public."

-**Challenge Negative Thoughts:** Replace "I'll embarrass myself" with "I am prepared and can handle this."

-**Break Goals into Smaller Steps:** Start by speaking in front of a small group, then gradually increase the audience size.

-**Seek Support:** Join a public speaking club where you can receive constructive feedback and encouragement.

- **Visualize Success:**Picture yourself confidently delivering a speech and receiving applause.

-**Take Action:**Sign up for a public speaking course and attend the first session.

Embracing Goal Setting for a Thrilling Journey

Setting thrilling goals is a powerful way to enhance your self-esteem and create a fulfilling life.

By understanding the importance of goal setting, creating S.M.A.R.T. goals, and overcoming fear and doubt, you can embark on a journey of personal growth and achievement.

Remember, goal setting is not a one-time activity but an ongoing process. Continuously review and adjust your goals as you progress and evolve.

Celebrate your successes, learn from your setbacks, and keep moving forward with confidence and determination.

Embracing challenges is essential for personal growth and building self-esteem. Life is full of obstacles, and how you handle them can define your journey.

By adopting a positive mindset and practical strategies, you can transform challenges into opportunities for growth and success.

Thriving in Adversity
Adversity is a part of life that everyone faces at some point. Whether it's a personal setback, a professional hurdle, or a difficult situation, adversity tests your strength and determination.

Thriving in adversity means not just surviving but growing and evolving through tough times.

Accept the Situation: The first step to thriving in adversity is to accept the situation for what it is.

Denying or avoiding the problem only prolongs your struggle.

Acceptance allows you to face reality and start finding solutions. It's okay to feel upset or frustrated, but accepting these feelings as part of the process can help you move forward.

Stay Positive: Maintaining a positive attitude can significantly impact how you deal with challenges.

Focus on what you can control and look for the silver lining in difficult situations. Positivity doesn't mean ignoring the problem; it means approaching it with a hopeful and constructive mindset.

Seek Support: Don't be afraid to reach out to friends, family, or support groups. Sharing your experiences and feelings can provide comfort and new perspectives.

Sometimes, just talking about your problems can make them seem more manageable.

Take Action: Instead of feeling helpless, take proactive steps to address the challenge.

Break down the problem into smaller, manageable tasks and tackle them one at a time.

Taking action, even small steps, can boost your confidence and sense of control.

Learn and Adapt: View adversity as a learning opportunity. Each challenge can teach you something valuable about yourself and your abilities. Adapt to new circumstances and be open to change. Flexibility and willingness to adapt are crucial for thriving in adversity.

Practice Self-Care: During tough times, it's essential to take care of your physical and mental health. Eat well, get enough sleep, exercise, and practice relaxation techniques.

Self-care helps you stay strong and resilient in the face of adversity.

Learning from Failures

Failures are often seen as negative experiences, but they can be powerful learning opportunities.

Every failure teaches you something valuable and brings you closer to success. By shifting your perspective on failure, you can use it as a tool for growth.

Redefine Failure: Instead of viewing failure as a defeat, see it as a step in the learning process.

Every successful person has experienced failure at some point.

It's a natural part of taking risks and trying new things.

Analyze Your Mistakes: Take time to reflect on what went wrong.

Analyze your actions, decisions, and the circumstances that led to the failure.

Understanding the cause of your mistakes can help you avoid them in the future.

Extract Lessons: Identify the lessons you can learn from your failures.

What can you do differently next time?

How can you improve your approach?

Use these insights to refine your strategies and actions.

Stay Persistent: Persistence is key to overcoming failure.

Don't let setbacks discourage you. Keep trying and stay committed to your goals.

Remember that failure is temporary and success often comes after multiple attempts.

Celebrate Effort: Celebrate your effort and courage to take risks, even if the outcome wasn't as expected.

Acknowledge your progress and the fact that you are willing to step out of your comfort zone.

Seek Feedback: Ask for feedback from others to gain different perspectives on your failure.

Constructive criticism can provide valuable insights and help you improve.
Be open to suggestions and use them to grow.

Building Resilience
Resilience is the ability to bounce back from adversity and keep going despite challenges.

Building resilience strengthens your mental and emotional fortitude, helping you navigate life's ups and downs with confidence and grace.

Develop a Growth Mindset: A growth mindset is the belief that your abilities and intelligence can be developed through effort and learning.

Embrace challenges as opportunities to grow rather than threats.

This mindset fosters resilience by encouraging you to persevere and learn from setbacks.

Build Strong Relationships:Strong, supportive relationships provide a safety net during tough times.

Surround yourself with people who care about you and offer encouragement.

Lean on your support network when needed and be there for others in return.

Practice Gratitude: Gratitude helps you focus on the positive aspects of your life, even during difficult times.

Regularly reflect on what you're thankful for, and express gratitude to others.

This practice can boost your mood and strengthen your resilience.

Stay Flexible: Flexibility is a crucial component of resilience.

Be willing to adapt to changing circumstances and find new ways to achieve your goals.

Flexibility allows you to navigate obstacles more effectively and stay open to new possibilities.

Set Realistic Goals: Set achievable goals that challenge you but are within reach.

Break larger goals into smaller, manageable steps.

Achieving these smaller goals builds momentum and confidence, helping you stay motivated.

Develop Problem-Solving Skills:
Strengthen your problem-solving skills by tackling challenges head-on.

Approach problems methodically by identifying the issue, brainstorming solutions, and implementing a plan of action.

Effective problem-solving enhances your ability to cope with adversity.

Take Care of Your Health
Physical and mental health are foundational to resilience.

Maintain a healthy lifestyle by eating well, exercising regularly, and getting enough sleep.

Practice stress management techniques such as meditation, yoga, or deep breathing exercises.

Reflect and Learn: Regularly reflect on your experiences and what you've learned from them.

This practice helps you gain insights and build on your strengths.

Use reflection as a tool to grow and improve continuously.

Stay Optimistic: Optimism helps you maintain a hopeful outlook, even in tough situations.

Focus on what you can control and look for positive aspects in every challenge.

An optimistic mindset fuels resilience by encouraging you to keep moving forward.

Seek Professional Help: If you're struggling to cope with challenges, consider seeking help from a mental health professional.

Therapy or counseling can provide valuable support and strategies to build resilience.

Thriving Through Challenges
Embracing challenges is a powerful way to build self-esteem and foster personal growth.

By thriving in adversity, learning from failures, and building resilience, you can transform obstacles into opportunities for success.

Remember, challenges are an inevitable part of life, but your response to them defines your journey.

Adopt a positive mindset, seek support, and take proactive steps to address challenges.

Use failures as learning experiences and stay committed to your goals.

Build resilience by developing a growth mindset, maintaining strong relationships, and practicing self-care.

With these strategies, you can navigate life's challenges with confidence and emerge stronger and more self-assured.

Practicing self-care is a powerful way to improve your self-esteem and overall well-being.

Self-care is also another word for word for Self-compassion,it [1]involves treating yourself with kindness, understanding, and forgiveness, especially during difficult times.

Understanding Self-Compassion
Self-compassion is about being kind and understanding to yourself when you're going through a tough time, just as you would be to a friend.

It means recognizing that everyone makes mistakes and that you're not alone in your struggles. Self-compassion has three main components:

---

[1]

Self-Kindness: Being gentle and understanding with yourself rather than harshly critical.

Common Humanity: Recognizing that suffering and personal failure are part of the shared human experience.

Mindfulness: Holding your painful thoughts and feelings in balanced awareness rather than over-identifying with them.

Practicing self-compassion can help you cope better with life's challenges, reduce anxiety and depression, and enhance your emotional resilience.

Overcoming Self-Criticism
One of the biggest obstacles to self-compassion is self-criticism.
Many people have an inner critic that constantly judges and belittles them.

Overcoming self-criticism involves recognizing these negative thoughts and replacing them with more compassionate ones.

Pay attention to the negative things you say to yourself. Notice the tone and content of these thoughts.

Question the validity of your self-critical thoughts. Are they based on facts, or are they exaggerated and unfair?

When you catch yourself being self-critical, try to respond with kindness. For example, if you think, "I'm so stupid," counter it with, "Everyone makes mistakes, and I'm doing my best."

Also develop a habit of speaking to yourself in a positive and encouraging way.

Use affirmations and gentle reminders of your worth and capabilities.

Practicing Kindness

Being kind to yourself is essential for self-compassion.
Treat yourself with the same care and understanding that you would offer to a close friend.

Do something kind for yourself each day. It could be as simple as taking a relaxing bath, enjoying a favorite book, or spending time in nature.

Let go of past mistakes and forgive yourself. Understand that everyone makes errors, and what's important is learning from them and moving forward.

Acknowledge and celebrate your achievements, no matter how small. This helps reinforce positive feelings and boosts self-esteem.

Mindfulness and Self-Compassion
Mindfulness involves being present in the moment and accepting your thoughts and feelings without judgment. It's a crucial

component of self-compassion because it allows you to observe your experiences with a balanced perspective.

Mindful Breathing: Practice mindful breathing by focusing on your breath.

Take slow, deep breaths and pay attention to the sensation of breathing.
This helps you stay grounded and calm.

Body Scan:
Perform a body scan by paying attention to each part of your body, starting from your toes and moving up to your head. Notice any tension or discomfort and allow yourself to relax.

Mindful Reflection:
Reflect on your day mindfully, noting any moments of difficulty or stress. Instead of judging yourself, approach these reflections with curiosity and compassion.

Self-Compassion Exercises

Incorporating self-compassion exercises into your daily routine can help you build a more compassionate relationship with yourself.

Self-Compassion Break: Take a few minutes each day to give yourself a self-compassion break. Place your hand on your heart, take a few deep breaths, and say to yourself, "This is a moment of suffering. Suffering is a part of life. May I be kind to myself."

Compassionate Letter: Write a letter to yourself from the perspective of a compassionate friend. Describe your struggles and offer words of comfort and support.

Loving-Kindness Meditation: Practice loving-kindness meditation by silently repeating phrases like, "May I be happy, may I be healthy, may I be safe, may I live with ease." Extend these wishes to others as well.

The Role of Forgiveness
Forgiving yourself and others is a critical aspect of self-compassion. Holding onto grudges and regrets can harm your emotional well-being.

Acknowledge Your Feelings:
Recognize and validate your feelings of hurt or anger. Understand that it's okay to feel this way.

Let Go of Resentment:
Holding onto resentment can weigh you down. Make a conscious decision to let go of negative feelings towards yourself and others.

Forgive Yourself:
Understand that everyone makes mistakes. Forgive yourself for past actions and focus on what you can do better in the future.

Practice Empathy: Try to see things from the perspective of the person who hurt you.

This can help you develop empathy and move towards forgiveness.

Embracing Imperfection
Perfectionism can be a significant barrier to self-compassion. Embracing imperfection involves accepting yourself as you are, with all your flaws and strengths.

Recognize that no one is perfect, and it's okay to have flaws. Embrace your imperfections as part of what makes you unique.

Avoid setting unattainable standards for yourself. Set realistic and achievable goals that allow room for mistakes and growth.

Instead of striving for perfection, focus on progress. Celebrate the small steps you take towards your goals.

Building Resilience Through Self-Compassion

Self-compassion strengthens your ability to cope with challenges and setbacks. By being kind and supportive to yourself, you build emotional resilience.

Surround yourself with people who encourage and support you. Having a strong support system can help you stay resilient in tough times.

Prioritize self-care by taking care of your physical, emotional, and mental health. Regular self-care practices help you stay strong and resilient.

Maintain a positive outlook, even in difficult situations. Focus on what you can control and look for opportunities to grow and learn from challenges.

Creating a Self-Compassionate Mindset
Developing a self-compassionate mindset involves shifting your perspective to one of kindness and understanding towards yourself.

Start your day with positive affirmations that reinforce self-compassion. For example, "I am worthy of love and kindness."

Regularly reflect on your strengths and positive qualities. Remind yourself of your accomplishments and the things you like about yourself.

Developing self-compassion takes time and practice. Be patient with yourself and acknowledge your progress along the way.

Integrating Self-Compassion into Daily Life

Incorporating self-compassion into your daily routine helps make it a natural part of your life.

Start your day with a few moments of self-compassion. Practice mindful breathing or say a kind word to yourself.

Keep a journal where you write about your experiences with self-compassion. Reflect on your progress and the challenges you face.

End your day with a self-compassionate reflection. Think about any difficulties you faced and how you can be kinder to yourself in the future.

Practicing self-compassion is a powerful way to enhance your self-esteem and overall well-being.

By being kind and understanding to yourself, you can navigate life's challenges with greater ease and resilience.

Remember, self-compassion is not about being perfect but about accepting yourself as you are and treating yourself with the kindness you deserve.

Strong relationships are like the backbone of our lives. They support us when we're down, celebrate with us when we're up, and give us the strength to keep going, no matter what life throws at us. For women, building and maintaining healthy, strong relationships is crucial for self-esteem and overall well-being. This chapter is all about understanding the importance of relationships and how to nurture them in ways that lift you up, not bring you down.

The Importance of Strong Relationships

Let's start with why strong relationships are so important. Humans are social beings—we thrive on connection. Having people in your life who genuinely care about you, who see your worth even when you don't, can make all the difference. These are the people who remind you of your value, who encourage you to keep going, and who stand by you through thick and thin.

When you have strong relationships, you're more resilient in the face of challenges. You know you're not alone, and that gives you the confidence to face whatever comes your way. Good relationships also contribute to your self-esteem. When you're surrounded by people who love and support you, it's easier to see yourself through their eyes, to recognize your own worth, and to believe in yourself.

Trust and communication are the foundations of any strong relationship. Without them, it's hard to build something that will last.

Trust is about knowing that someone has your back, that they won't hurt you, and that they'll be there for you when you need them. But trust isn't something that just happens—it has to be earned and maintained. To build trust, you need to be reliable, honest, and open with the people in your life. If you say you'll do something, follow through. If something's bothering you, talk about it instead of bottling it up.

Communication is key to understanding and being understood. It's not just about talking—it's about really listening, too. Good communication means being open about your thoughts and feelings, even when it's hard. It means not just hearing what someone says but trying to understand where they're coming from. When you communicate well, you can resolve conflicts, deepen your connection, and build a relationship that's strong and healthy.

Recognizing and Valuing Your Support System

Your support system is made up of the people who are there for you no matter what. These might be family members, close friends, a mentor, or even a supportive partner. Recognizing who these people are in your life is important because they're the ones who help you grow, who support your dreams, and who pick you up when you fall.

Take a moment to think about who these people are for you. Who can you call when you're feeling down? Who believes in you even when you don't believe in yourself? These are your people—cherish them. Let them know how much they mean to you, and don't be afraid to lean on them when you need to.

But remember, relationships are a two-way street. It's important to give as much as you receive. Be there for your loved ones when they need you, support them in their goals, and show them that you care. When you nurture your relationships this way, they become stronger, and so do you.

Setting Boundaries in Relationships
While strong relationships are vital, it's equally important to set boundaries. Boundaries are about knowing your limits and communicating them clearly. They're not about shutting people out—they're about

creating a healthy space where you can both thrive.

Setting boundaries might mean saying no to things that drain you, or it could mean taking time for yourself when you need it. It's about being honest about what you can and can't handle. Remember, it's okay to put yourself first sometimes. You can't pour from an empty cup, so taking care of yourself is crucial.

When you set boundaries, you're telling others that you respect yourself, and that you expect them to respect you too. It can be tough at first, especially if you're used to putting others' needs before your own, but in the long run, it leads to healthier, stronger relationships.

Building Relationships with Yourself
One of the most important relationships you'll ever have is the one with yourself. Before you can build strong relationships

with others, you need to have a strong relationship with yourself.

This means treating yourself with the same kindness, understanding, and respect that you would offer to a friend. It means taking time to get to know yourself—what you like, what you need, what your goals are. It means forgiving yourself for your mistakes and celebrating your successes.

When you have a strong relationship with yourself, you're better equipped to build strong relationships with others. You know your worth, you know what you want, and you're less likely to settle for less than you deserve.

Every relationship faces challenges—there's no way around it. But it's how you handle these challenges that determines whether your relationship will strengthen or weaken.

When conflicts arise, it's important to address them head-on. Avoiding problems only makes them worse. Instead, approach conflicts with a spirit of understanding and compromise. Try to see things from the other person's perspective, and work together to find a solution that works for both of you.

Sometimes, relationships go through tough times. You might feel distant from a friend, or you might have a disagreement with a family member. During these times, it's important to remember why the relationship matters to you and to be willing to put in the effort to mend it.

Letting Go of Toxic Relationships
Not all relationships are healthy, and sometimes the best thing you can do for yourself is to let go of a toxic relationship. Toxic relationships are those that drain you, make you feel bad about yourself, or keep you from growing.

It's not easy to let go of someone, especially if they've been a big part of your life. But staying in a toxic relationship can do serious harm to your self-esteem and overall well-being. If a relationship is causing you more pain than joy, it might be time to re-evaluate whether it's worth holding on to.

Letting go doesn't mean you've failed. It means you're choosing to put yourself first, to create space in your life for relationships that uplift and support you.

Nurturing Strong, Healthy Relationships
Building strong relationships takes time, effort, and a lot of love. But the rewards are worth it. When you have strong, healthy relationships, you have a support system that lifts you up, helps you grow, and reminds you of your worth.

Remember, the most important relationship is the one you have with yourself. By treating yourself with kindness and respect, you set the foundation for all the other relationships in your life.

Your career is more than just a job—it's a significant part of who you are and how you contribute to the world. For many women, our careers can be a source of pride, fulfillment, and even identity. But they can also be a place where doubts creep in, where the weight of expectations feels heavy, and we're finding our voice can seem daunting.

Overcoming Imposter Syndrome

Let's start with a term that too many of us are familiar with: Imposter Syndrome. It's that nagging feeling that you don't really belong, that you're not as competent as others think you are, and that it's only a matter of time before you're "found out." It's a feeling that can be crippling, especially for women who are breaking new ground in their careers.

But here's the truth—if you've ever felt this way, you're not alone. So many women, no matter how successful, struggle with

Imposter Syndrome. It doesn't mean you're not capable or deserving—it just means you're human.

The first step in overcoming Imposter Syndrome is recognizing it for what it is: a lie. It's a voice that tells you you're not enough, but it's not rooted in reality. You wouldn't be where you are if you didn't have the skills, the intelligence, and the determination to succeed. So when that voice pops up, challenge it. Remind yourself of your accomplishments, the hard work you've put in, and the unique qualities you bring to the table.

It's also helpful to talk about these feelings with someone you trust. Sometimes, just hearing someone else say, "I feel that way too," can be incredibly validating. Knowing that even the most accomplished women feel this way can help you see that Imposter Syndrome doesn't have to define you—it's just one part of the journey.

Developing Leadership Skills

Leadership isn't just about being in charge—it's about influence, inspiration, and guiding others toward a shared goal. Whether you're leading a team, a project, or just leading by example, developing leadership skills is key to thriving in your career.

But here's the thing: leadership doesn't look the same for everyone, and it doesn't have to. You don't have to be the loudest voice in the room to be a leader. In fact, some of the most effective leaders are those who listen, who empower others, and who lead with empathy and understanding.

Start by recognizing the strengths you already have. Are you a good listener? Do you excel at problem-solving? Are you the kind of person who others turn to for advice or support? These are all qualities of a great leader. Leadership is as much about who you are as it is about what you do.

Next, focus on building the skills that will help you lead with confidence. This might mean developing better communication skills, learning how to delegate, or even taking risks and stepping outside your comfort zone. Leadership is a journey, and it's one that you can grow into over time.

One of the most powerful things you can do as a leader is to lift others up. Whether it's mentoring a colleague, advocating for someone's ideas, or creating opportunities for others to shine, leadership is about more than just your own success—it's about helping others succeed too.

Creating a Thriving Work Environment
A thriving work environment isn't just about the physical space you work in—it's about the culture, the relationships, and the way you feel when you're there. It's about creating a space where you and others can do your best work, where you feel valued, and where your contributions are recognized.

If you're in a position to influence your work environment, start by thinking about what you need to thrive. Do you need more flexibility? Better communication? A stronger sense of teamwork? Whatever it is, don't be afraid to advocate for it. Sometimes, creating a thriving work environment starts with a simple conversation about what's working and what's not.

Building a positive work culture often starts with small, intentional actions. It could be something as simple as acknowledging a colleague's hard work, celebrating small wins, or making time for regular check-ins with your team. These small acts can build trust, foster collaboration, and create an atmosphere where everyone feels motivated to do their best.

It's also important to take care of yourself in the process. Burnout is real, and it can sneak up on you when you're trying to do it all.

Make sure you're taking time for self-care, setting boundaries, and asking for help when you need it. Thriving in your career doesn't mean sacrificing your well-being—it means finding a balance that allows you to bring your best self to your work, day in and day out.

Thriving as a Woman in the Workplace
Thriving in your career is about so much more than just climbing the ladder—it's about finding fulfillment in the work you do, building meaningful relationships, and staying true to yourself along the way. It's about knowing your worth, trusting in your abilities, and not letting fear or doubt hold you back.

As women, we face unique challenges in the workplace, but we also bring unique strengths. We bring empathy, collaboration, and resilience. We bring the ability to see the big picture and the determination to get things done. By overcoming Imposter Syndrome, developing your leadership skills, and creating a work environment where you can thrive, you're not just building a successful career—you're paving the way for others to do the same.

Remember, your career is a journey, not a destination. There will be ups and downs, but with each step you take, you're growing, learning, and becoming the best version of yourself. Keep believing in your potential, keep pushing forward, and know that you have the power to create a career that not only fulfills you but inspires others too. Let's continue to thrive together.

In the hustle and bustle of life, it's easy to move from one goal to the next without pausing to acknowledge how far you've come. But celebrating your achievements is so much more than just patting yourself on the back—it's about recognizing your growth, appreciating your efforts, and building the confidence to keep moving forward. In this chapter, we'll explore why it's important to take the time to reflect on your journey, the power of self-recognition, and how to plan for continuous growth.

Reflecting on Your Journey

Let's start by taking a moment to look back. Think about where you were a year ago, five years ago, or even ten years ago. Think about the challenges you've faced, the hurdles you've overcome, and the goals you've achieved. It's easy to forget these things when we're so focused on what's next, but your journey is filled with milestones that deserve to be acknowledged.

Reflecting on your journey isn't just about looking at the big wins—it's about recognizing the small victories too. Maybe you had a tough conversation at work that you were dreading, but you handled it with grace. Maybe you stuck to a new habit, like exercising regularly or spending more time with loved ones. These moments matter because they're the building blocks of your growth.

When you take the time to reflect, you're reminded of your strength and resilience. You see how much you've grown, not just in your career or in your skills, but as a person. You realize that every step, no matter how small, has brought you to where you are today.

The Importance of Self-Recognition
As women, we're often taught to be humble, to downplay our successes, and to put others

before ourselves. While humility is a virtue, it's equally important to recognize and celebrate your own achievements. Self-recognition is not about bragging—it's about honoring the hard work, dedication, and perseverance that have gotten you this far.

When was the last time you truly acknowledge your achievements? When was the last time you said to yourself, "I did that, and I'm proud of it"? It's easy to get caught up in what you haven't done yet, but celebrating what you have done is crucial for your self-esteem and motivation.

Self-recognition is an act of self-love. It's telling yourself, "I see you. I see the effort you put in, the sacrifices you've made, and the challenges you've overcome." It's about giving yourself credit where credit is due. And you know what? You deserve that. You deserve to feel proud of the person you've become and the path you've carved out for yourself.

So, how can you start recognizing your achievements? Start by writing them down. Keep a journal or a list where you jot down your accomplishments, big or small. This simple act can serve as a powerful reminder of how much you've done. It's something you can look back on whenever you need a boost of confidence or a reminder of your worth.

Planning for Continuous Growth
Celebrating your achievements doesn't mean you stop striving for more. It means you take a moment to appreciate how far you've come before setting your sights on what's next. Growth is a continuous journey, and planning for it with intention and purpose can help you keep moving forward.

When you think about your future, what do you see? What are the dreams you haven't yet achieved? What skills do you want to develop? What areas of your life do you want to focus on next? These are the questions that can guide your growth.

But remember, growth doesn't always mean reaching for something bigger or more prestigious. Sometimes, it's about deepening your understanding, improving your well-being, or nurturing your relationships. Growth is personal, and it should be aligned with what truly matters to you.

One of the most effective ways to plan for continuous growth is by setting intentional goals. These goals don't have to be monumental—they just need to be meaningful. Think about the areas of your life where you want to grow, and set goals that challenge you while also being achievable. And don't forget to celebrate each step you take toward those goals.

As you plan for growth, be kind to yourself. It's okay if your journey takes longer than expected. It's okay if you take detours or change directions. What matters is that you keep moving forward, at your own pace, in a way that feels right for you.

Embracing the Joy of Achievement

Celebrating your achievements is about more than just acknowledging what you've done—it's about embracing the joy that comes from knowing you've grown, you've learned, and you've persevered. It's about allowing yourself to feel proud and fulfilled by the progress you've made.

As intentional women, it's important to recognize that your journey is unique. No one else has walked in your shoes, face your challenges, or experienced your victories. So, give yourself the recognition you deserve. Celebrate every step you've taken, every goal you've achieved, and every lesson you've learned along the way.

And as you continue on your journey, keep in mind that growth is a lifelong process. There will always be new goals to reach, new challenges to overcome, and new achievements to celebrate. So, take it one step at a time, cherish each moment, and never stop believing in your ability to thrive.

Let's keep moving forward together, celebrating the amazing women we are and the incredible women we're becoming. Your journey is worth celebrating, and so are you.

So here we are, at the brink of something truly amazing—your future. Can you feel the excitement? This is the part where everything comes together, where you take all the strength, confidence, and wisdom you've gained and step into the next chapter of your life.

Your journey to building self-esteem has been full of ups and downs, but every challenge you've faced has shaped the incredible woman you are today. Now, it's time to embrace your new self, maintain that high self-esteem, and share your journey with others who need inspiration.

Let's start with a little moment of reflection. Take a deep breath and think about who you are right now. Not just your name or what you do for a living, but who you *really* are. You've grown so much—you're stronger, wiser, and more confident than ever before. And it's time to fully embrace this new version of yourself.

Embracing your new self means letting go of the doubts and fears that once held you back. It means looking in the mirror and truly loving the person staring back at you. You are worthy of all the good things that life has to offer. You've worked hard to get here, and it's time to own your journey.

Sometimes, embracing your new self can feel a bit strange, almost like you're stepping into a new pair of shoes. But with every step you take, those shoes will start to feel more and more like they were made just for you. Don't be afraid to stand tall in them. You've earned this, and the world is ready to see the full, unapologetic version of you.

Maintaining High Self-Esteem
Now that you've built up your self-esteem, the next step is to maintain it. Think of self-esteem like a beautiful garden. You've planted the seeds, nurtured them, and now they've bloomed. But to keep those flowers blooming, you need to continue tending to

your garden. This means practicing self-love every day, setting boundaries, and not letting anyone or anything diminish your sense of worth.

Life will still throw challenges your way—that's just how it is. But now, you've got the tools to handle them. When doubt starts to creep in, remind yourself of everything you've overcome. When you face criticism, whether from others or that little voice in your head, stand firm in the knowledge that you are enough. Maintaining high self-esteem isn't about never feeling low—it's about knowing how to lift yourself back up when you do.

One of the best ways to keep your self-esteem high is to surround yourself with positivity. This might mean spending time with people who uplift you, engaging in activities that bring you joy, or even just taking a few minutes each day to remind yourself of your strengths. Whatever it looks like for you, make it a non-negotiable part of your life.

Inspiring Others in Their Journey

Here's the beautiful thing about your journey—it doesn't end with you. Every step you've taken, every struggle you've overcome, has the power to inspire others. There are women out there who are facing the same challenges you once did, and your story could be the light that guides them through their own dark moments.

Inspiring others doesn't mean you have to stand on a stage or write a book (though you absolutely could if you wanted to!). It can be as simple as sharing your experiences with a friend, offering encouragement to someone who's struggling, or even just leading by example. When other women see you living your truth, they see what's possible for themselves.

You have so much to offer the world. Your strength, your wisdom, your kindness—these are gifts that can change lives. So don't hold back. Be open, be generous, and most importantly, be yourself. You never know who might be watching, who might be silently cheering you on, or who might be finding hope in your story.

Stepping Boldly Into Your Future

As you move forward into your thrilling future, remember this: you are not the same person you were when you started this journey. You've grown, you've transformed, and you've become someone truly extraordinary. Embrace this new chapter with open arms, confident in the knowledge that you are capable of achieving great things.

Keep nurturing your self-esteem, and don't let anyone dim the light you've worked so hard to ignite. And as you continue on your path, take the time to reach out to others who are on their own journeys. Your story has the power to inspire, to uplift, and to make a real difference.

This is just the beginning of something incredible. Your future is wide open, filled with possibilities, and the best part is, you get to shape it. So step boldly into it, with your head held high and your heart full of love and pride for the woman you've become. This is your time to shine, and the world is ready to see you in all your glory.

Let's continue to walk this path together, with strength, courage, and an unshakeable belief in ourselves. Your thrilling future awaits.